Gentlemen in Turbans, Ladies in Cauls

JOHN GALLAHER

Should we have stayed at home,
wherever that may be?

—Elizabeth Bishop, "Questions of Travel"

SPUYTENDUYVIL

ISBN 1-881471-75-6

Spuyten Duyvil
http://spuytenduyvil.net
1-800-886-5304

For Wayne Dodd

Acknowledgments

American Letters & Commentary: "In Motion & in Repose"
Borderlands: Texas Poetry Review: "Ritual For Fall"
Denver Quarterly:
     "Cocktail Party at a Summer House"
     "Patination Estuaries"
     "In the Book of Telling Stories"
FIELD: "Gentlemen in Turbans & Ladies in Cauls"
For Poetry (www.forpoetry.com):
     "Eolian Processional, Oak Ridge"
     "Only What Happens Disappears"
     "Of a Three Dimensional Object on a Flat Surface"
     "Comings & Goings at the Park on Sunday"
Indiana Review: "The Odalisque on the Obelisk"
The Journal: "Durational Issues"
LIT: "Olduvai Gorge Bon Vivants"
     "In the Orrery with Carol Anne"
The Ohio Review:
     "A Walk Around the Pool Thinking Thoughts"
     "The Sky Is Blue & Birds Fly Through It"
Sulfur: "The Attractions of the Attractive"
West Branch:
     "Notes   The Time Spent Falling"
     "Notes   What She Brings to History"

Thank you to all those who aided in the composition of these poems, and to Michael Heller, judge of the 2000 Spuyten Duyvil manuscript competition. And for all, Robin.

CONTENTS

How the Sky, Where the Earth

Preterite for Missing Bodies

In Tableau Vivant

Studies In Midair

Where the Sky, How the Earth

From Where One Is to
Where Everything's Just the Same

It's a day on the lake in July, eighty degrees and sun. OK,

let's just say it's a project
                              of getting (a certain clarity, geometries
of light) from point A to point B, this fine

prospect of living proof. (Prima facie,
the whole point

of departure.) So alley-oop
from there to here (all of a piece),

the ground, the residuum, coming up to meet you
                                                    (aground).
The ground,
abuzz with rumors of any two people.

Call them points A and B.
It's a beautiful day in Austin, on the lake, say.

There are sailboats, white and red.
                                        Should we move

to point C then, have one turn to the other
with a scent of detail (*It was a beautiful day when . . .*),

or back to point A sub-something?
Rehearse a better departure? (*. . . setting off from shore*)

Sitting close, the lineaments of her cheek,
and the green and the blue . . .

Because it just came to mind, and
Avail yourself. It'll be a beautiful day on the lake. Sailboats

(you've to dead reckon, one
would hope, vital stuff) on a beautiful day,

turning,

a line with two dots,
as one speaks and to whom

the local colors of local things.

Only What Happens Disappears

Two people begin at the door, beginning,
as we say, in the midst. A corridor

is disclosed between them, and each
starting out, two nights

down a corridor. These somewhat intricate
and protean developments. Two

dilemmas walking
into the park's dark,
                    and the curve of muscle up her leg

behind. Each turning, then (& the light
across her chin & shoulder), each

being, and the sticky little leaves
of spring, as two (crepuscular) walking. She and, say

he, strolling (this Jill,
this Jack) and his dark socks
                    with yellow diamonds (&

the opossum in the sassafras tree).

She and the piquancy of the poplars,
receding (& the scarlet tanager)

In the Book of Telling Stories

She's been sitting here, where once upon
a once she's recalling it

as trailer and repeatingly.
                          They left

the door open
for the mist for the dust

mixed in the paint. She has the windows open, where
she's been sitting here.

Who paints a floor anyway.

———

Deciding to end
                at the door

he ends at the window
open on the lot. Desiring reality she says leaving she says

evening. And then rain and them
getting somewhere, listening

to the chance staccato of a delivery truck's
left turn signal.

———

The evening being even being fair, he finds it easy
going. Being a park
                    apart. Some things they put together some things

approaching gray: Texas sage.
                      Being here or the evening

where meanwhile suddenly
                        the story's who tells
the story. Black cutouts of sky.

The Sky Is Blue & Birds Fly Through It

Air is air.   —Stevens

> The bark of philosophy
> across the idle prairie, rose
>
> as birds rise
> on an early fall afternoon,
>
> to return but not
> to return often
>
> in the dwindling afternoons.
>
> And the birds, startled
> by the cry of their passing,
>
> passed over
> to a clearer spot
>
> a bit farther along.
>
> All the idle afternoon
> across the idle prairie.

Cocktail Party at a Summer House

1

Approximating the certain
disturbance of the given, several people

are in their lives in a room on Bay Shore.
There's a vase with flowers.

And if one should call the vase
cut crystal
        and the flowers spring tulip,

must one then wonder
at the way the drapes
are more gray than taupe and drawn?

And then if several should, with one voice,
                       turn
saying We are alone, should one

remark the chairs
are bleached wood

and one pulled back against the far wall?

2

Approximating the lawn is to stand
at the picture window

and be standing at the picture window.
The apprehension is going. The red tulips.

It's Saturday and the rest
of the day is spring. And then

one remarks the distance: a picnic on the shore,
the yellow, the green reach, and sky—

or rather this one day, this breeze, when leaving's
what staying's all about.

In Motion & in Repose

The feeling she should be doing something
else, more: the sand,

the girl playing with the red ball, attitudes of wind
and grass. For someone else, pursuant

to the ocean before her,
                              waves broken
on pauses. Her shadow

resembles herself taller
and more slender, or pools

between her legs. It's the middle of the season. Sand.

So she's on a beach pursuing a red ball,
blue stripe. Skipping through the tide

that extends as we keep forgetting it extends
and the scrub grass that interferes

with beach access (the vista view). The red ball

arcs a line between thrown
and caught (her derring-do). She's turning

the beach to form (as derry

& nonny), and plays a song against
                              surf (boundary
conditions). A solitary

shadow's revolving. A red
ball spins, reflects waves without

sound, a diverting
                    choreography. Stripe and stripe, we fade
past grass to a girl on a beach (little company)

playing with a ball. And sand,

the parabola, return (the lengthening
repetition of a single pattern).

The History of Tourism

There are no people
in this evening, their gestures
                       (the numerousity)
like similes, up one side
of the block and down,

full, then over
full with summer. This thought

we had while out walking the other

evening, that Tuesday was
Tuesday's contacts,
                as concept
and/or percept, eddied about, perforce,
as this door's red

as that one's white. We
always enjoyed waving. And the hedges.
(Holly & Laurel.)

And we've had three dogs now
and seven cats, the break
that continues
            (& Providence
their guide), as we were

deciding
         between jacket and sweater
and the streetlights popped on (the diurnal

round) to fix
and hum
        (in camera), sluing
the static compositions,

thirty-seven houses surrounding our house, half
dissolved in night.

Durational Issues

1

Late summer cresting
                    through the blue salvia and shale break. He's certain
as he kneels there. Late summer. She's sure

as she turns (as he reaches [as she folds backward,
the afternoon all up about them],

certain of nothing the body won't enclose),

these rhythms of wax and wane (askance). And how the
white delphiniums, how the impatiens, burgeoning

(astride), keep
in the current (the dotted line

of shoulder
to hand at the back), working the math of

hand on shoulder: hand
at the small of the back, fingers

joining the palm near the wrist.
How they arch toward an image, the yard

all up about them, this acervation
(skin & gist), this accession—

2

They're on the lawn as it begins to rain (the wicker, the trowel).
They are on the lawn and it's raining, a tempo

in a burst of wind. An equal lift from porch
to quilt (certain, their eyes meet)
                                    as the clouds break, the sun's aureola

catching the pulse of her inner elbow
in the frost of the little gold hairs, a

mist of sweat on her upper lip. Sweat

playing down her spine (*equate*, say,
say *attend*), a procession

without measure, clouds
and the idea of clouds.

Local Time Among the Particles

Preparing for a party, this one
flutters and this one
                        huffs. They hover

over this and this. It's evening, the living room's
in fine shape, from speaker

to speaker. (*Nice clothes*, Robert says.) Wheeling all things
through all things. All

aglitter, the vestibule, what they're looking over
(for good measure), these

active parties. We'd sit out so
all evening, objects of fixed

duration. Blithe (the complete equipage), and keeping
our own council. We've something to do

with volume, form. All of us

————

nice couples, then, household items

working the invisible, the recto and verso
(of all things, a cutting). Being

as we're ceremonious people. They debate
the dip and bowl, the collocation. We debate our chips,

while the evening attenuates
                              to the pith and spin
about the atrium, astir

with great views to dine by, a dilection.
The water freezing

then melting. Various weights
in motion on a field.

The Difficulties One Works for Backdrop

He tried everything as he went looking,
on the double, in Riverhills. When she lost
                              her part, her parcel, she went off,
in Springhollow, lickity-split.

So that's it then, in sum and ensemble. Enough for them: he goes
left and she goes left. Great strides

and wobblings. Great wan
and scion. In Glendale, one

mixes rooms with her passing, her dispatches
and itineraries. In Meadowbrook,
                              walking from fluxes to flows, one goes
from nexus to fulcrum, with the driest point
                              of pointing.

That's one way. Perhaps
the way. So keep
                your eye on the clamor, *in extremis* you might say,

talking in skullduggery terms (pettifogging, we'd
addend), for argument's sake, this
special grade of people in this special circumstance

(so one may twaddle & garnish—
so one may dawdle in bad deportment—) at arm's length.

In Arborcreek, Laurelridge, such small places
                              unmarshalled,
such catch as catch can,

making the trip

Two Action Poems

NOTES *the Time Spent Falling*

She's written. It's not what things look like,
a feeling or a moment
                              (at the door,

on the porch). Not the enterprise nor recognition
they've talked so much about

falling before their depictions
by afterthought. By semi-gloss. In chambray. She folds

a bit of paper (before the mantle, the sheer) on which she's
written something. The paper's canary yellow
                                                    with green

lines. She works
the folds to half and quarter (so

they're looking
at themselves in profile). Carefully to eighth

and sixteenth. Who she isn't
                              looking at who
she won't be, an idea (she's folded

a bit of paper from margin to margin)
                                        that won't come closer
than the opened window

(at times this yearning), the will
to form these lovely people (these mimes & tumblers)

disappearing until
their gestures follow.

She's raising a glass of water
(raising a glass in a room
                    before the bay window

in a season between seasons) to her lips.
She's using her left

hand as her image
fragments in a glass of water
                    in this enlarging season,

escaping the attendant day,
the lucent windows,
                    by increment. Of her own

curios, this very self
in beveled glass.

She's looking
around the room, between

the hall mirror and bay
window. A mere rise of open ground

with a few gray houses dotted over it,
comes to her, embossed

(& where are we
                    looking, now that we're no longer
looking?). With the weather

outside (a present),
she's lifting a glass of water and the room lifts

sensibly, all
about the room.

PRETERITE FOR MISSING BODIES

Composure on East Fourth

The Big Apple, as the advertisements
tell you, surrounds. *Snow.* It snows (it's

snowing). This's

about something, be assured (from
the subjunctive to the conditional). The sphere

of the absolutely real, as light
                              and color in the open air. Living
it up, as the odd

man out (Frank & Bob), attempting the mechanics
of a chili dog (& thinking of a friend), to see beyond

the mundane
              biographies of this place. This world of places
and menageries,

where there's no whole,
only discrete objects (the thinkable chili & cheese). *If I*

were you and *If it stops snowing.* The solace
of the indistinct, under snow. Unburdened

of memories, they
and their judgment/imagination/perception
                                          /faith
board a bus to Times Square,
on Saturday, to master these things. Some of them

are dining off to your left (I meant
dying, of course), the locals
in regional costume. This

completely new going about, it goes

a long time like that (may it suit
                              your circumstances), attempting

surely, and with conviction (Bob & Frank),

a chili dog and a beer—
early in the day, still. And the sun on your

side of the planet, and
all those wild years

The Attractions of the Attractive

1

They're attending the grass
where the sidewalk

joins, and attending the several
doings of day, the aquamarine, the swing

set and exigency (the domain & mnemonics).
Piecing

the park together, a sequence
of dears, whence and whither,

serpentine
in apposition. And the pleasures dally

in the arbor, the half world
in dollops, egg and dart (the acclivity,
                                            declivity).

2

The colored balloons go off
at once

and the blues and the reds
and the yellows go off

a priori in April. Without apologies,
doddering for this

and that, exeunt
severally, the colored balloons.

The apricots the redolent
bristling with ardor,

of equilibrium at their apogee,
attendants in light,

go off. Categorical and stacking
as the plethora as the quorum

as the lullaby halve
the surface and the straining,

the epistle the firmament go
in April in Appertain.

3

A search has commenced
                    behind
the one counting

by ones. Little bodies scattering, busy,
the yard spreading

all around. And one says look

and they all look
saying Up saying Up

with a certain flavor
(carrot grass, mint leaf).

And the bodies in light
turn in the grass

each parallax.

Busy no bulwark on my republic
busy no coterie on yours.

A Walk Around the Pool Thinking Thoughts

Among the extracts from the Palace
of Afternoon, we find ourselves

playing cards on the patio. Woo-hoo, we

call in unison, waving to the ambiguous
wilderness, happy as clams

for all that. And all we have
are ways of putting it. The way

Debra's hoping for something
other than incessant beginnings, as she

tells us, for one. And Blaze

wanting a haircut, walking a sure walk, with clever
and clear lines, within the life of forms

on the Bikini Atoll. Take my word for it, there are
many ways to use a swimming pool. Like that moment

Tom decided to define a word without a dictionary.

For example, I define the word "red" while
going to the snack machine. I define the word "a-diving-

board" while surfacing. This might as well

be a good idea. This might as well be everything
behind them for the time it takes

to dry off. All these awkward bodies.

And I thought I knew something
about cards, but look at this mess. (You've always been there

long enough to leave.) It's a sure winning bet,
the scene we're always approaching,

the life of perpetual Saturdays.

Pajama Party

Maybe this's across town. Or all over
                                       town.
Everything's leafy and the lawns are mowed. It's night,

etc., etc. . . . these girls, this room

full of hairstyles. And what
should they recall
                    of the dogs

barking, off and on? (*Beings Animaculus*, Melissa says.) Being

as they'll want
                  to recall (later, when they've
gone [collating & collation], or mostly) games,

attempting to call up
spirits, light as a feather
                       and stiff as a board. Attempting
the half bath and vanity (What's that

book about you're reading?), poco a poco
                             down
the evening, feeling all gangly. The pool

emptied, they're watching
a TV show. There's a house (a they). It's an adventure show,
here, with the obligatory
                    brother and his
glass to the wall.
              (We're just sitting here, right?)

And they don't like the temperature. And
they don't like the streetlight
casting a big X through the room. Where late

from the pool (as refraction), and therefore summer
peeling them like onions, these several girls
(at eleven, at twelve) and

several notions (as objects held in the
light, & turned). Jackie says

she's knowing things, she says
it's self explanatory, after all. As they say things

for greens, say hope
                    for know (the skedaddle & seriatim), pulling
the blinds. And later

they're abed (the protocol), surveilling
                                        this flavor
of moving about, higgledy-piggledy. Freezing panties.
And mum's the word.

Deportment in Public Places

The whole evening and cloudy martinis.
Where, past lavender, past sage (or perhaps
Janice & Phil & you & me beside

the white dresser), the idea

of a butterfly enters the room. Well?
We fell or we didn't fall (fronted, &
musicked, & deportmented). Are we

doing OK? Or is that a bit of
ancient history? (*By our deportments
& carriage in all actions.*)

I was turning off the radio. The room,

hardly in better shape, what
with purple martins all along the walls,
eminent and pecuniary, utterly put away. And perhaps Janice

and Phil and you and me. And the idea
                              of a butterfly up

from the cadmium and semi-gloss. (*The
room was full of women . . . many of them
in faire deportment unmasqued their faces.*)
                              Ah, inexorable

exurbia (a scrim). That's what I'm here
for: to put you
                    at ease, one would have one
of us say, seething with our settledness.

As they're looking to the window

behind the fuchsia, running the matins,
which opened with great fanfare. And yes
Janice and yes Phil and yes you, yes.

It's black and white and the people look small.
But we were all smaller in those days (*in
the character of a dancing-master,*

*in which capacity we gave a lesson
                              in deportment*).

Comparisons of what to ourselves? (Compared
to ourselves we've outdone ourselves?) A
butterfly, perhaps, as an idea

that enters a room. (*Thank you, & Let's
rate the creatures, the good
            and bad beasts.*) This locus. And Janice and Phil and you
and me. This's what I'm asking (I call this

a conversation). And we return, we

return to the whereness of everywhere,
                              this ground of effects,
perfectly perfunctory. The wallpaper
we desire? *Thank you.*

Each wall? *Thank you. Oh thank you.* (*As illustrated by
the deportment of both ice & bismuth
on liquefying.*) The whole evening and

cloudy martinis.

In the Orrery with Carol Anne

Now would be a wonderful time
for abstraction: unimaginable

others, and a good afternoon (&
harebrained) to sate

the best fittings and fixtures, which are
our essential strategies of survival. And hairdos.

This's the system getting complex, I guess. As in
the poetic moon and the scientific moon

enter a hall, time
permeates the carpet. (Or space as an image

of a world view [somewhere
'tween above & below].) As in the myth worked long

in Mesopotamia. The myth
eventually moved to Columbus.

The myth moved next door. Worked on the lawn.
And the planets do their planet things, field

mice scattering (their ratiocination).
Things are not as they were, apparently. In tide, in tidings.

The wind blows the curtains across the counter, rolls
the moon to the closet (these accidents

which are expected & certain to occur [as the
modalities of motion]). So, Carol, no

details matter (not these
that are not those; not those

that are no longer [the regents & galvanometer
{mere galvanic encouragement}]), here,

where we recognize ourselves (*our frail original,
& faded bliss*), to reconvene
                              by afternoons.

Decembering

—faith in the easement

The seven shadows of the child
regarding the imperfect

reflective silver, cavil (their Entrance & Exit)
as the parking
            lot, eventide, East Meadow, sings
in rows of mothers

and fathers (meinie & meiny). They've made
a list, quick

with occasions (austere

streets & verdant shrubbery), of Saturdays
with bells (these embellishments) gaveled out

in primary salutations, attendants swaying
in white,

in yellow. Cadre
of this child in produce

singing this market. Flora,

fauna, and fresh
and gracious light singing Open
sesame, with

season of all seasons,
between (Lucy & Stephen) two aisles, toothsome
ditties, fugitive pieces. Presently

clambering forth (the mien event), the young
married couple is and
                  the cute young
married couple is (the wold

dancing out) swinging by
for a few things, banners
held up

by wire
in no wind

Place & Object

A valley puffed in early summer,
and this mad rush to the ridge,

some boys are following a creek, waist
deep. It's Alabama (1975), a junked car

and dull water. It's the earliest of summer,
and morning glories

with three boys (busy,
                              this chorus), noodling
their way (what they want to be)

up river. It's the stretching up
of shadowed green on their right and left, stretching (what a valley

might mean) indistinct, mint to gray

and splashing through Alabama (their geometry & striped
shirts [white & blue]) with their sneakers on, fashioning the banks

with flotsam, with jetsam. And since nothing
                                            happens (the same
things differently), they wade, these abstractions

of boys in water, from a day
                              where having nothing
happen is all (arriving), and then up. Now,

shoes left out
on the rock? It's the last thing over the valley, as we're turning

back (a parade of possible color
& three boys) with this gloss, enough to be

as far as they go, our favorite objects, living
their actualities,
                    longer days then shorter days.

The Building's What Surrounds the Building

A product of happy peoples, the happy
towns (the plinth) composed

the houses that dot the beach
and cling to the earth. All their lives

building heaps of sand, sitting
on heaps of sand. And here,

watching so closely (the clever girl, the capable
fellow), one sees it's different

than what it was, an interior,
the multiple surfaces (events). The eventual houses.

———

Was that a flight of imagination?
To lift in answering files, your old kit bag?

(Dissembling, the entryway
& the atrium, the element
                    within which's you [dwelling],

as recreation system, as promenade.)

And the beach that goes up
in a fine thin line,
weave of the distance between,
                    digging (& we're off)

a very entertaining heap.

———

                    So the pleasant people
composed of streets and houses,

of walls and vaults, a site, tincture

of the landscape moving through the landscape. Happenstance?

Remonstrance? So closely watching this one
thing, efflux (all this busy cure),

we will have been done
                              (a palisade?).
And your little sand bucket
                              and your little sand shovel

Olduvai Gorge Bon Vivants

They're on this teeter-totter
and having a good time,

saying one time ablution
and one ablation.

They're on top
                    and on top.
The mechanism chafes a bit.

They remember where they've been, and
are bound repeating it

in the plurality of afternoons
of Saturdays

of summer. (Thick or thin.)

The playground shifts red
then blue

from this teeter-totter
with squeaks and giggles.

The Qualities of Known Quantities

How America has Detroit to plan its obsolescence, twelve blocks
hoping no pieces of buildings fall
on passers-by,
                   a monorail that won't

come smooth. (Detroit's imagining itself
an escarpment, & the quintessential
building
         along for the ride.)

So we're making a road trip to the nineteen twenties,
                          hoping structure's a good way
to keep from thinking about the body,

as good as a sixteenth-floor cornice,
or frieze, or vestibule and doorman,
                     as perturbation, as

excursus. This mausoleum's thinking
of ourselves, asking the use
                   of twelve blocks of Detroit
without commerce, meaning (the arbitrament,

the syncope).

It's your own *Hello?* that comes back. My own
How do you do?

And thinking of myself

there. Imagining I'm in an agreeable mood.

Imagining you're saying something.

When You Look Down the Ground's Coming Up

She's seeing herself at the Met
on a bench, between two heavy breathers. (must we, this site)

In situ (sort of
a step by step thing), she's seeing the patrons before her

regarding the animal kingdom behind them,
                                          wandering off.
A lot of width.

———

Does she hear the rustle of papers, the squeak of shoes,
the several contexts?
                    (going to museums & things like that)

Have they gotten her into the picture a little more deeply?
(*as red, as blue . . .*) The breathers and so forth.

———

So where's she going
in this picture. Looking at herself

(Perhaps she'll get this bronze plaque beneath her. [Perhaps.]) with these

two heavies counting paintings, one
one, one, at the Met
                    side by side. With *Watch out,
the next one's coming,* one could guess,

———

this ambulant circularity, these austerities
                        in some direction,
one folds over as. Maybe it's supposed to be like that, the ratios

all there, more
or less,
        the breathing story in mid career.

Our own little bench going around.

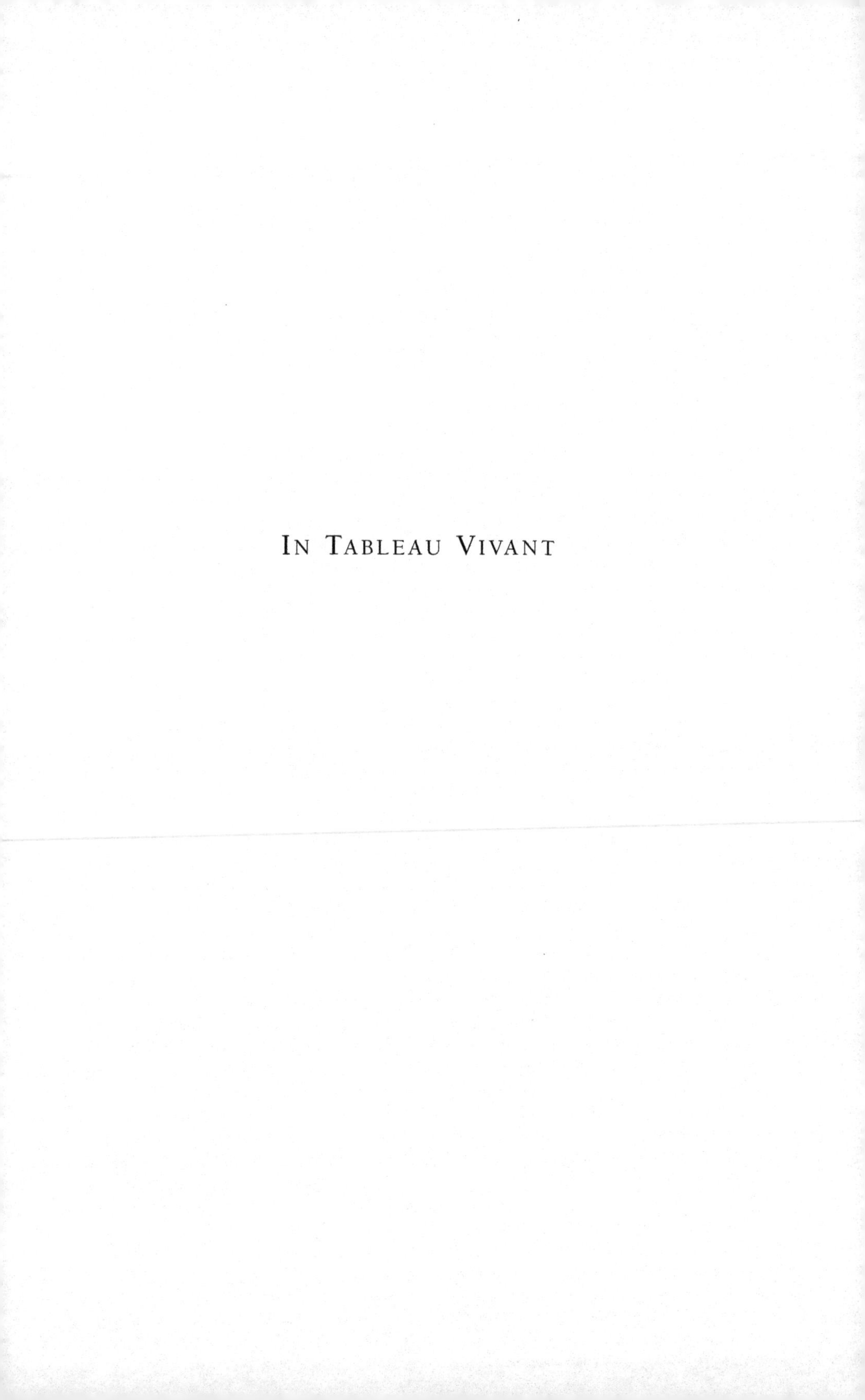

In Tableau Vivant

Eolian Processional, Oak Ridge

One taking off her clothes

and another singing about it.
There's a competition

of violets, white and yellow
(singing to close

the day about them).
How one hobbles oneself

for stillness. And still,
with what isn't there

for support. Several yellow
tulips and several red tulips

(one taking off one's clothes).

How one
stills oneself, spring

and a sudden
ochre and amaranth,

the window and lounge.
One singing. (The green.)

The green looking
so much closer than the trees.

The season's gone to seed with two
                              watching themselves (as the trailings
of absence) in the sayable orchard, contained

as if the house . . . (as if the cage escapes the bird)
its ornate extensions
                    at the ineffable.

They're all that's left — self (singular)
filled with moving, the predictable

/the unpredictable, a cage
as if cage matters (plural),

as if someone's always paying
attention and oppositions

natter and clutch

[. . .]

in this only middle.

How certain things appear. A peach orchard.
This copse and bird, jade and azure.

A good memory helps, Julie's saying. Or at least
a jacket and coffee . . .

At some point we do something. That for each form
                              (the qualities
of the not absent), its formulæ (as these figures
move without),

clattering in neat rows of bare trees

(*Turning into the wind
with my new best friend—*)

with little darkness
and little light

Vestiges of the Endeavor

Things in themselves (several things
to attend to), the surrounding

of familiarity, fetter

the figure by the bed
and the figure at the window.

We won't reduce the other and we must,
where there are perhaps two figures

locked in what two figures are. And still (this clutter)

one turns
toward you, the sheets patterned

with burgundy, with tan. One turns sure (some augury, some
divination) of birds

on the ridge
and this living in circumstances, congeries
and conjuncture,

positional information, with matters clamoring. "Throng"

you say, you say "worldly," figuring on the bed
or figuring by the window

(the indiscretion of objects).

Praise of the Seasons

The image of herself surfacing
                              that she's diving into
is startling her,

in the still dark rising of Palmer Lake.
Water all the way from her to not-her, the length

of the pier
in the shadow of the pier (avant),
and her fanning out (between Remmel

& Tiffany) to herself, breaking form. Going
for a walk, she goes for a swim

each afternoon (a trice), and here this girl
in a two-piece rushing up. Down

to this causerie then, with a rim of aspen
                              and pier in dark color.
The sky. Left here
                  at the end of the dock,
projecting (herself)

days that come (to
water) and go

Documentary Landscape

A house bordering a wood, insofar as
two lovers are in the kitchen
speaking of kitchens. A treatise on architecture

and the decorative method. Two indoors. This

could begin a story
or end one. This could be the center
                              of a story. Two people
regarding the space between them
(thriving). An inquiry into conceptual thinking.

What could be there,
and lovely, remains
                    ejecta, a conception

of the external world, taken indoors by the stereo.
One has one's tongue to the tongue
of the other.

We'll picture these two lovers
                         naked in the afternoon
as we read about them. We're at the
sink filling two glasses with water. The window looks out

on dogwoods. On geometry in four dimensions,

mingled with a crowd of others,
in the kitchen, at the
                    window. Facing the bobolinks squarely.
What good would questioning them do.

At the sink filling two glasses, one turns
the faucet on and one
holds the glasses, by turns, beneath the stream.

The stereo's on the dresser. The stereo's on. These lovers
all afternoon, an atlas of anatomy
                              for artists. A likeness

the sun plays out
over the silver and glass. It rains. And evening coming on.

Aviary Precepts

The roof arcs down
to where a small group of women is milling. On the back lawn,

they're speaking quietly of the lawn, in print dresses.

They mill right to left, geranium
and hibiscus, with the crab grass milling about

a note of exhaust and the lawnmower from over
the fence (screen or screening device).

Egrets are more a problem this year than last, this
solid underfoot. This, we'll call it vesicle,

how it makes its appearance (grommet & grotto).

Perhaps the weather's turning
early, with the wonderful demarcations. Greta, well yes,

between two perennials. So which gate
will you take?
          (Will you take a gate?)

(Maybe the house, maybe dodging the house?) This hint
of moisture (egress, ingress). The mower

from over the fence (the
white fence). Patterns

from taupe to mauve
as a small group of women turns

Patination Estuaries

We saw the seeing of her, there at the boat races.

And what else could we call it? Forgetfulness?
            The teal sea? (While watching
embarkation, disembarkation?)

Very neat, at the boat races.

And when she will have given enough, watching
            the boats (there at the boat races). For whose sake.
            For the lee and weigh.
For the sake
            of convenience.

She was setting out for the water. She had this blanket reserved
            for the occasion, the several blankets
for several occasions.

A little excited now, nothing missing. And waiting at the finish.

She and her parasol, everywhere beginning (quick,
            like otherwise).

And she can't forget it for you, there at the boat
            races, bearing up to resemblance.

An adventure she escapes and doesn't escape,

waving the bright boats on.

Ritual for Fall

To say you're sad isn't enough.

You must add the girl
reaching for daisies, in a gown of daisies

while over by the veranda, flicking matches,
others dance,

separating her from perhaps
herself,
          darker, looking down
at undifferentiated gray clasped hands.

Only this: marble
for an instant, she looks down.
                              And these clay

faces line in a row on the veranda
overlooking the flat ocean.

She's reaching for daisies, a pirouette (the moon

casting a pillar across a wide
expanse, not
                making the shore) as

they're looking out over the sea, sensible from a distance,
to where the moon's reflected

larger and more white,
sorting the ambiguous splotches of their moments

from occurrence
                to instance.

Of a Three Dimensional Object on a Flat Surface

As they lie in bed just now
listening to the wind working
the eaves, she catches him following the curve
of her shoulder.

He was just having this dream where he was
in that tree in the backyard,
the lines for what she really meant swelling up
all around him. His right

hand touching *Nothing More Than*
and his left how *Hope
Fills With Swallows.* Naming the long thin morning (the alterity

& bramble) "Everything that's not me
is in doubt." And how she thinks, now,
                              that looking

is falling to a plateau and ladder,
the sorts of things that go with

how eventually they'll rise and do something
with the windows. He'll go for the toolbox.

And they'll lose
track. That memory's waking in different places
constantly, like a child.

Like disinterested behavior.
Blankets as topography. Her hair.

Comings & Goings at the Park on Sunday

So it's really about the flat surface
and the covered back — intimations

everywhere, divined as one divines
such things

as the fullness of a body
missing all over town. Sunday painters, mutable

with the last one looking
who looks at the signs beginning

to catch and shifts changing
on the square, not weather nor salt. A person looking

for a person and the evening easing
down (mere

referentiality), incarnadine — to a seam,
flattening the canvas as it recedes

— as the weather takes
(things in light) over. Enough

that Sunday's only moving,
and to dwell

(gala & exegesis
[what we think's what we think

we've seen]), a person
before the park's

wall, heightened in the gloaming,
as the last of the sun sparks mica

from the dull concrete
to a field of stars.

Delta Admonitions

Here, the edges of things. Here, the thrush and linnet on the quay
in this late summer heatwave (a time, a hitherto apropos).

She's regarding the water, moseying
between accrue
                 and ecru,

in shadow. She'll launch herself

in that direction any minute now (channeled,
in this dash to the water,

teeming because she's thinking of it,
while making
                 from slip to slip), parts that go

to one's organization (fillip/abscond), parts that go
to the ocean spreading out alarmingly.

So this girl, at past
midday, germane to weather

(& many other divides as well), is
crossing over (forward,

which's out) the pier, the watermark (lines
of demarcation), on her way.

And sometime later different things
                 (a wealth of changing hues).

The Economy of Parameters

She comes to a thought at breakfast, over coffee,
that her ideas about the wild, the untidy

fecundity, don't comment past the drawn
blinds (How'd they get so yellow?). This dawn

she marks that'll never be enough, this December,
this January, ticking an order,

over coffee and toast. As if all her ways
of saying winter were just to say

spring coming, a silver bowl
at the center of her unimagined table. A thought

she comes to over breakfast, passing between the frost
skirting the kitchen window

and the bowl of apples on the table, that to go
is to return (this meanwhile),

the trees (excitable as the yard) turning
(these fields she's not played in for years), and

a bowl of oranges on the table. Each morning,
after coffee, she'd open her door

(she decides [these fields]), where this
morning a world glistens

in first frost and landscape.
(One last look over her shoulder.)

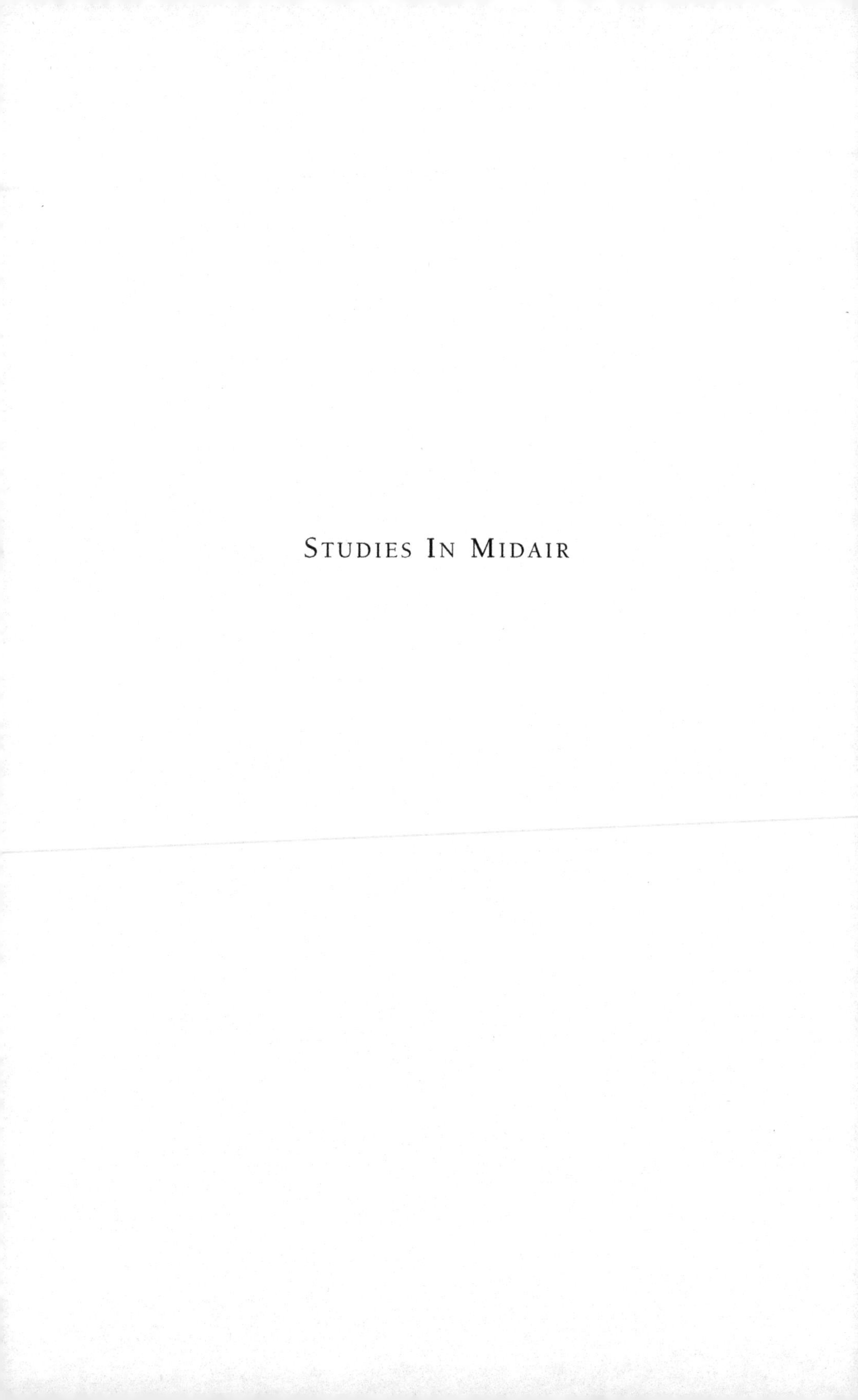

Studies In Midair

The Possibility that This Is It

It was a splendid evening, if
memory serves,
                 a pool filled with not flowing, more or less.

It was fine and granular, saying only that
                              I want to be saying
(anent cerulean), all this business of the elements.

We were all right, it was
evening (pagoda & chateau): we were driving.

Remembering more than we knew, we were
pointing (there is) and pointing (there was
                           [point to point]).

And the horizon recedes as one approaches. Julie
was less sure than that. Of course, Tom said.

You can stand here or here, Orion clear
but missing some stars, with the boulevards
                               accumulating.

Evening and the mask of heaven: evening
                        (suppose this): suppose
this matters to you suppose, carrying your points with you.

This, the comity of balcony and pool where late
                          and loudly
the lures of story, the allure (& Julie, & Tom).

It was (all things counter) splendid, the evening: clouds
or not clouds: movements of wind;
                 the slow dropping away of each neighborhood.

The Vertigo of Common Places

Daddy, how big is a airplane's tire?
Is it as big as me?

1

Let's just say it's a house
on Maple Street in June and aren't the tulips something?
Let's just say it's what the oath's for,

how they put
reclining angels on tombstones
(off & busy angels)

and that there's something moving
over the plain
far off

and receding
(one foot in myth & one
on green earth). Let's just say

it's a long way to be here, the oath of June
and Maple, and we can't
quite tell what's not left to tell,

as the apex is exhaustion, and then
he's an old man and he dies
looking up and swearing he hears something.

2

The catastrophe that is, as one would
have to be, refuses to redo it, the head
raises its defiance, a last . . .
                              concrete pixies and sunshine, and
barely through the shrubbery,
how it's over or it's all over or at least

unsure (common
ailments for bodily functions &/or decoration).

I've this house on Maple and tulip, the more
to collect and codify,

strewn together, accumulating.
And an airplane flies over.

3

To know at the outset that flight
is chromatic (& well organized)
allows for how, with propeller sounds and arms

out over the lawn,
there's plenty of room to maneuver:

a young couple's selling a house
and buying another house. A man's selling
the house his father died in.

My parents buy a house and later
I sell it to a young couple
who sell their house to buy it.

So then my father anoints himself
hurriedly because he's growing
larger, soon he'll be bobbing to the surface, soon
his shirt puffed out behind him like a parachute

as he's flying in the body
of his brother who died descending
toward Southeast Asia
55 years ago. It's a telephone call what did it. And him growing
late and cold.

Whenever possible
we fly. And through an otherwise blank afternoon.

4

A man's grown all soft and rather dizzy
on the divan beside the front wall heater. He's thinking

chronology doesn't help him feel any better
now that he's trying to place it on shelves. If only

he could sell more houses. Maybe two.
Something on the west side. Yeah, something on
the west side and the telephone rings

that maybe something on the south side (which isn't

the west side, & yet?).

Let's just say he says that "Immersed in the facts of my life,

I've forgotten who I am."

Carbon Lullaby

Returning from looking at something far off, one sees the trees
scuttling the outside wall. It's easy

to say December extant. It's easy to say
the year's ending,

Into the despond of (So we doff our caps?),
as one returns from Orion's belt thinking (By dint

of persiflage?) a man's walked
from the back yard, after a heavy rain, and has taken

the yard with him.

And aren't there more stars now?
And why aren't there more stars
                                in the argot, in the aggregate, now?
(These white dots of extremity.)

Fresh from what was (standing in the kitchen looking out

on the back yard), he's at
the window without his father risen. How one waits
                                and then waits no longer,
all faces, evinced, all forces. He's returned without

his telescope from the box elder trees, from the night sky,
from December, the back-

and-forthedness
that distance never catches. Say it's altogether

capricious, the way the stars work (we say 'akin,'

'arrayed') far off. That poverty
by which one lives.

On the Affection of Inherited Forms

With two impatiens
                    in bloom and two not, to whom
should I refer you (our contents)? To whom the toaster

and breadboard, whom querying the accidental, the
authority of
a chance thought, an island in the kitchen,
                              a nice place to wait? Maybe arboreal

and how they're able to think
and how they're able to act? These bodices and codices

suggesting air down
plenitude and O, like finding
a house and ringing the bell. First ducking past

the cedar. Anon. (First ducking the juniper. Agon.) Through
the grass
          darkly, as

ergo and aegis, like closing a door and opening a window, this technical
work. I made the block
and realize it's colder now (this axis), with several

alikes and unlikes tapping each
other, anywise or fundamental, in the window box. One object
                                                    moving
(one orbit)

faster than another, one mailbox, one sprinkler (erst). One car (car),
as well red's more
                    meaningful than green,
noticing at the corner it's turned colder (ersatz). This day of otherwise

mostly good news.

This field of what this field becomes.

Study in a Figure of a Landscape

So what does this resemble? I'm sitting in a field the other day. So

I'm sitting in a field the other day which
is a little dickering with perforce

and furthermore (as in all resemblance,
limit). But I can't

sit without
thinking there must be a field. Which is

that there must be some trees
and one must be more slender (something moving quickly from
side to side).

Does that set the scene? This vista? This overlook?

———

I'm holding it out for your edification.

———

Perhaps something shoots and springs?
All right, to coil and recoil, something shoots and scours,

a monster looking up from a plate to listen.
But I can only startle so far

knowing it's the field
that's the initiate: sitting's an afterthought. As well scouring.
And monstrosity.

As is I, with distance beginning
to set in. Pale trees mingling

to sky, where we're talking resemblance, not idea. Taking notion,
a very soft bed of field.

————

So here's the theory: let's not
do it shall we, this monster? This

field of What, which makes it

impossible past resemblance, this field turbid about a field
of stars, where we light. A field telling us how to talk

amongst ourselves. How to say tall grass showing off a fall
breeze.

————

Spore and beetle (facets that don't contribute to shape), in a field
abraded. All that cutting for composition (how much pressure
                                        before the twig

snaps). Okay, so I'm not in the field. Pick your way.

But what does the containment look like?
(this field of stars

that you're tilting your face toward) Open your mouth,
I can see you better this way. North, between dogwood and oak.

————

But this is monster isn't it.

————

This monster,
with what catches the ear (rustle of grass, twig snapping),

knows the primary occupant is
field and the subject is

composition: a monster in the woods
as you're picking berries. Maybe a raccoon?

A raccoon with these hands. Maybe you

———

in a pleasant valley with a picnic site,
set to with pin lights

from a field guide. "I had to go here,
the words took me." (North.) Let's say

I'm throwing these spots over my shoulder

with gears, as if you're fecundity
and fields, addition, confetti. Field

and monster in an orderly and mannered way:
fuzzy stellar objects (between dogwood & oak).

———

Maybe you add white space.

———

Spore? Beetle?

———

And the main direction's out. The crickets, lulling

(this machinery), and specks for eyes. Maybe this, set to
with refraction.

"Let's look
for berries before we head back," you say (half a moon).

———

See what's coming?
Wasn't it inevitable to the composition? A wide

field of clear survey. Direction.

Something into vivisection, polished. Polished,
it's been polished to an edge. It has a tripod and gears.

———

It's clinical stuff: now, a field, underbrush rustling.

For the Burning Field
—A rhetoric

1) Instructions for the History of Writing

Beginnings must be small, letters perhaps. Perhaps a piece of music.
A trumpet.

Then a leader; then a guide.

Introduction: *I want to tell you a story,* or
A watershed happens every twenty years.

I want to swim in the river because desire is key.

The simplified title: I intend to shelter myself from the waves and
from the smoke.*

Then the comfort of the trivial:
    science fair projects in which you (as signifier) put one bean
    plant behind yellow tinted cellophane, one behind blue tinted
    cellophane and one behind green tinted cellophane.

In the beginning God creates whatever
    which is the center of something because it's the center of some-
    thing. History's its own argument.

A helpful characteristic of the trivial is stage directions, maybe
Exit left, pursued by bear.**

Then someone says Let's do that, then Let's do that
    because the words aren't the thing.

"I never thought dirt was much of an issue either," Someone could
    say enigmatically in the protagonist's ear at dinner,

"Or an intense spiritual experience over my spaghetti." It's like playing

----

* see Homer
** See Shakespeare

Twister, the luminous history (the golden thread) that breaks
        for a way out of its perfection. As in
Creation's getting repetitive.

You can see it going,
        curious.

2) *How to Live in the World*

A slight woman on the ferris wheel
waving to another.

Accepting her derivations takes time, she says (excepting
the rising keening of splitting air)
                                    in red and white. I'm going

to try each one, she says for us. She continues
this way (hello
             /hello), over
the arcade and county organization, all evening. Busy making up

the difference (or making out

her house & his), she's making herself
                                    busy. Someone's trunk
is opening. Distant clapping. Say

whirligig then, on the observation wheel, his right hand

at her wrist, desire
or desire's cessation. A gesture, say. Here in The Silver

World, and to bestir oneself, she's
an evening where X and not Y. And several

departures later, another
in deep terrain
                is looking up (to give a certain direction
to one's sight) with a hot dog

and a wave et cetera, redolent at the fairgrounds. A little

burned on nose and cheek, she's
in slate blue, in white, in spring
                        yellow, with the humming of

the spheres. The hub-bub (& all of A are B). And what else
for her? By the arcade, the ring toss? All
                        white, all

red from the ferris wheel (toy cars on toy roads), a
cameo in yellow brocade
                        flits by. A slight woman,

inchoate, circling.

3) The Odalisque on the Obelisk

And I was thinking crazy that's what I was thinking,
which is as good an explanation as any. So
I saw the sunrise this morning
and a woman jogging with her dog. What can one do

to make up what happened? Say
Lunging dog: lunging dog: dog sitting down? Say
an action continues until
it continues no more? Maybe the day

at twelve hundred and fifty miles an hour
over the Appalachians. And the night
at twelve hundred and fifty miles an hour
over the Appalachians. In the face

of thinking I might as well be the dog.
And then when I curl beneath her feet

we both might as well forget it. We might
as well marry
                    or begin collecting plants. As in *The day,*
The night, The mountain. As in it's all about

none of that because it's never
about what it's about, where I strike

up a conversation and pat
the dog, the *Labrador Retriever.* And we're not all alone

when we talk to each other
in the other history, the one that doesn't

happen. The inevitable

unknowable history
of certain incoherent utility. Rustic silence. So

I should've just said
The woman. I should've just said *The touch.*

How movement's always only
an approach. How movement's always only against. Always only

leaving (the mountains naked in a manner
we can never be—)

and easing back.

A SEQUENCE: Vertigo of the Commonplace

Of Gloss & Marginalia

The solidity of a doorknob
as it turns, but

not just any doorknob, this beautiful
doorknob in the palm

with fingers in the grip
as if gripping a steering wheel, full hand

then, as enveloping a telephone receiver
and the fold,

how a roller coaster hovers
at perihelion, before . . . but

less obvious (depending
on who) to say

maybe closer to Christ's Why hast thou,
the great weightlessness

before anything (the shroud,
the temple) is rent

and earth rising ever

—gripping only nails—and simpler
still

at the doorknob
with the latch withdrawing

from its socket
merely

and past ringing

The Talk Between Rooms

She's thinking of the print,
she says. The almost rising of it

when the room's suffused with light (*A
kindling gleam of hope Suffused the Spirit's lineaments**). She's

saying perhaps. He's moving it (an interior
with figures) to the writing table, where the mirror would catch it
as one passes in the hall, interiorly. She's

thinking perhaps the hall itself, the white
and wood of it. Thinking it a crowded hour, how

the couch's blue mostly. And the chair,
burgundy. Something about the plants, the cat

(an assemblage of pigments), as well these
clouded eyes one imagines

looking back, to look at us looking. So that one
would want how one must, to step back, to see the identifiable
tableau. The votive and donated things. Or, in stepping,
to regard the movement (moving

people, the palaver [Telling her nursery
tales & palavering the little language

for her benefit.**]) between two rooms.
Here, they'll call it hall
                    and study. Here,

they'll call it print. And one would want them,
would want to climb into the picture

and lie down. All that space.
And all that space.

---

* See Shelley
** See C. Brontë

A Guidebook to Novels of Unusual Structure

It's my second time
on this page I know, but I don't remember getting here.
You spent some time there yourself
recently, with several thoughts? I heard. So how was it, and

tell us how
you do it? We asked of Miss Marshanetteipause. Miss
please-call-me-diamond, or platypus (for crying
in the sink). All these round characters.

The air there, of course, is subject
to availability. But this's not a problem, or much
of one anyway (the calm

of sentence after sentence). Not worth feeding
the cat over, as we say. Lunch and dinner,
their loudly respiration, these couples and singles.

(One could barely tell our lips moving.) April,

I believe, but I could be
talked out of it. They say: Have a drink? What can I get you? Several
is a good word to say
when you're not sure of what to say. With Seth

out in the back forty, I recall that much at least. Humming
a rumba, and the crop's in the field. Cuba, perhaps? Aruba? And
to top it all off, the roof's relaxed
                              and whistling softly . . .

These losses they practice, we practice in no
particular order. Anyway,
you will have been there a long time

by that time. That, yes, and their nearly complete opacity.

A distance safer, safer even
than grammar itself.

Gentlemen in Turbans & Ladies in Cauls

So these guys are laying bricks, ladies
and gentlemen, in the desert. A way

to spend the day, one supposes. Nice long desert. There.

And let's suppose that in this desert there's a palm. Some
to the left, and some

the right (so let's think about the desert this evening), these guys
biding their time in the volumetric background.

And they've palms to hit the palms (no clouds

all afternoon). Clippity-clop and habitual, they get up
real early, ladies and gentlemen. I can assure you, in the morning,

hitting the bricks. And after lunch they've all

afternoon. They know that
from A to Z, building

the land between this water and that water. Take this desert

for instance, call it A; and Z, could it in any way resemble a desert?
(Laying bricks & all that.) One cloud

maybe? And a brick's a brick's a brick . . . as in

There goes a brick of a guy. All cobalt and beige
in the desert air, this mantle and their materiel. Under

conditions. And here they didn't think

they'd like bricklaying at all. One might maybe even whisper
to one. When alone maybe. In the desert in our Sunday best

with straw and mud (all the fine ideas),

there's a palm. And it's getting on
toward evening, ladies and gentlemen.

We're going to the desert to lay bricks. We're going
to try and cheer ourselves up.

"In the Book of Telling Stories" is for anyone who's ever painted him-or-herself into a corner. It's also for Bin Ramke, for different reasons.

"The Sky Is Blue & Birds Fly Through It": the title comes from physicist Werner Heisenberg describing space, and then Wallace Stevens, not to be outdone, simplifies further.

In "The History of Tourism," "the numerousity" comes from Henry James in *Washington Square*, looking at Americans, while "Providence" owes itself to *Paradise Lost*, where Milton dubs Adam and Eve the second tourists, after Satan. "Farewell, happy fields . . ."

As for notes on "NOTES   What She Brings to History": "A mere rise of open ground" is Dorothy Wordsworth looking at the British countryside. Or maybe it's William.

The OED has much to say on deportment. "Deportment in Public Places" barely scratches the surface.

"Our frail original, and faded bliss" is from Coleridge.

"Decembering": John Donne, "A Nocturnal Upon St. Lucy's Day, Being the Shortest Day."

"The Building's What Surrounds the Building," or "The Box is Around the Box" is from *Learning from Las Vegas*, I think. If not, then ignore this note.

"When You Look Down the Ground's Coming Up": this little bit of helpful advice came to me when looking at the uncanny life-cast plaster sculptures of George Segal's that Robin likes so much.

Gertrude Stein defines America as a "space filled with moving."

"Documentary Landscape" owes much of its imagery to the books I've seen advertised in the backs of books.

"Ritual for Fall": Eduard Munch, in *The Frieze of Life*, adds the girl. The poem is for Kathleen Peirce.

"The Vertigo of Common Places": "one foot in myth & one / on green earth" owes its existence to J.R.R. Tolkien's *The Return of the King*, whereas the bit about forgetting oneself in the facts of one's life comes from a novelist I heard on Fresh Air in 1997. I forget his name.

"On the Affection of Inherited Forms": the line should read "Through a glass darkly," but why quibble?

"Study in a Figure of a Landscape" owes its title to Francis Bacon (though switched around a bit), and much of its method to Terence's camping trip.

"For the Burning Field," the title's derived from Charles Wright's "Looking Outside the Cabin Window, I Remember a Line by Li Po."

"How to Live in the World": truth be told, I think I got "the humming of the spheres" from someone. But perhaps to forget such things is how to live in the world.

"The Possibility that This Is It" owes a bit to Harold Bloom speaking of Wallace Stevens and the weather.

And finally, "Gentlemen in Turbans & Ladies in Cauls" owes much of its imagery to the liner notes to Neil Young's *Tonight's the Night*, ladies and gentlemen.

John Gallaher was born in Portland, Oregon in 1965. Just prior to his fourth birthday he was adopted, and has spent much of the last three decades living in various suburbs in Kansas, California, Alabama, Long Island, Texas, Arkansas, and Ohio. He studied at Southwest Texas State University (MFA) and Ohio University (Ph.D), where he worked for a time as Assistant Editor of *The Ohio Review*.

Made in the USA
Monee, IL
07 July 2026